COURAGEOUS LIVING FOR GOD

Daring Believer

Tameka M. Hacker

ISBN: 978-1-09834-854-0
ISBN eBook: 978-1-09834-855-7

Dedication

For

Mama Bear — Obviously, I love you more.

Papa Bear — Certainly, for the wise word or two.

Sibling — for the laughter, music, journals and friendship.

Last, but absolutely not least …

My sweetheart and husband, Gregory — for getting in
the car with me.

TABLE OF CONTENTS

INTRODUCTION

Even before I learned to read, I was enthralled with the beginnings of stories. Why? Because it was in the beginning that all was well. In the beginning was before the utter confusion, before the characters made mistakes or chose the wrong paths. At the start of each chapter, I didn't have to worry about the call to adventure, the long, arduous journey, or the great battle. It was safe inside those first two chapters, and no one ever strayed outside of the author's script. I did, however, begin to feel apprehensive in the middle of the story. As I turned more pages not knowing what to expect, I cringed at every wrong decision the main characters made. This is how it was in the Bible that I read, and this is how it was in my life. Now, looking back, I realize that God was doing His best work during the middle of my own story. In the middle of my disappointments, challenges, and triumphs, God remained by my side, leading me through life. Walking through my hometown libraries, I often wondered how many of my stories remained untouched and unfinished because I was too afraid to finish them. I realize now that this same regret happens as people allow the setbacks of their hearts to constrict them from walking with Christ. We can choose to remain safe and timid within our life stories' first pages or dare to journey with Jesus. The only way for a believer to reach the destination is to walk by faith through the middle of it.

It is often said in sermons that people are either going through, coming out of or about to run head-first into a storm. I've found on my journey that this metaphor's point is that life is always filled with swift transitions… but it's how you handle them that counts. The choices that you made in the past don't have to define who you are now or who you will be in the future. However, the principles that you live by today can shape your future. The character within the believer chooses daringly to press forward regardless of what comes their way. A believer knows that storms are terrible, but they wholeheartedly rely on God for deliverance. These storms may be people, places, or past or even current personal problems that come into our lives. God has a plan for our lives, but if we allow them, the storms will change our stories' narrative. True believers, however, will focus on Jesus during the storms of life. When choosing God, we decide that His Will and Way are the stories we want to live. Our only job is to trust and believe in God's promises.

If you ask me why I wrote this book, I will tell you that it was a decision to live out loud for my Lord and Savior Jesus Christ. When I took on the Daring Believer devotional, it was ultimately to inspire others to reflect on how to be braver for Christ than they would for anything else. We often read about other believers' courageous faith while shirking the possibility of us doing the same. There's a wide range of personal challenges that impede true, living freedom in Christ, and believers must fight them daily. This book will discover the personal effects of doubt, fear, pain, and loss in our lives and how they are overcome courageously with scripture. With ***Daring Believer,*** we are reminded that no matter the circumstances we encounter, God remains as faithful and inspirational as He always was. Just as God transformed the lives of those in the Bible, He's reaching out to us today. As you go through this devotional journey, I invite you to take notes on what you dare to do in your own life. Check where you are in your walk with Jesus, and dare dive deep into your relationship with Him. You can choose to live simply or be a ***Daring Believer…*** willing to journey in the right direction.

PART ONE:

Remember Who Called

Fear not, for I am with you; Be not dismayed, for I am your God. I will strengthen you,
Yes, I will help you, I will uphold you with My righteous right hand.

Isaiah 41:10

DAY ONE:

God Knows Best

Who has made man's mouth? Or who makes the mute, the deaf, the seeing, or the blind?
Have not I, the LORD? Now therefore, go, and I will be with your mouth
and teach you what you shall say

Exodus 4:11–12

Standing amid a miracle, Moses challenges God concerning that which is possible. He offers a list of obstacles and personal insecurities as justification for why God should choose someone else: "But, behold, they will not believe me, or hearken unto my voice" (Exodus 4:1) and "O my Lord, I am not eloquent… I am slow of speech, and of a slow tongue" (Exodus 4:10). Most of us ask God for clear direction in our lives, and here Moses stands questioning God's plan. While we may shake our heads in disbelief at how audacious it was for him to question God, the truth is we do it ourselves every day. At work, an opportunity for promotion presents itself, and we highlight the gifts of coworkers while denying our talent. A wonderful spouse could be beside us, but we aren't sure that we deserve their love. Not knowing what the future holds, we tend to let our negative inner voice pin us down. We lay out the reasons why we won't be successful because we don't want to have to face the *possibility* of disappointment. God reminds us who's in charge, letting us know that He is more than able to back those *daring believers* who are courageous enough to trust in Him. Knowing what is best, God won't let a negative perspective determine your outcome.

Lord,
When we get into Your midst, let us remember that You truly know what is best. Remind us to trust You and not the challenge in front of us. Only You have all the power to control the situation, so let us remain faithful to the word You told us. Let us not get in the way of the progress You want to achieve within our lives.

Amen.

DAY TWO:

You Are on His Side

And Joshua went to Him and said to Him, "Are You for us or for our adversaries?"…
So, He said, "No, but as Commander of the army of the LORD I have now come."

Joshua 5:13—14

In life, whether on a soccer field or the battlefield, most participants desire to win. Our hope is to be blessed to overcome every challenge which confronts us. More often than not, when we go it alone, we lose, but never when we go with God. When God calls us into a battle with Him, He assures us victory. He teaches us how to stand our ground and provides us a winning strategy. Amid the fight, we call on His Name and thank Him for His help. But when the battle is over, and we're rehearsing our victory speech in the mirror, there is a tendency to forget that Jesus is the true hero. The battle was His, and we were on His side. He *provided for us*, *defended us*, *fought at our side*, and ultimately *saved us;* so, soldiers, we must step out of the limelight and fall in line. We sing about the battle being the Lord's, yet how often do we give Him the glory? When you enlist in the army of the Lord, you must come to a straightforward understanding: whoever finds themselves on God's side wins!

Lord,
We are honored to be on Your side in this journey. Your methods
are unconventional. Your wisdom surpasses all, and Your victory
is certain. Correct us when we proceed, thinking that we are in this
walk for ourselves. Help us to remain humble when following Your
guidelines, even when it doesn't make sense on the surface. Give us
the confidence to go in what looks to be a circle around our prob-
lems until they inevitably fall.

Amen.

DAY THREE:

Jesus Walks with You

The LORD is my shepherd; I shall not want. He makes me to lie down in green pastures; He leads me beside the still waters. He restores my soul; He leads me in the paths of righteousness For His name's sake. Yea, though I walk through the valley of the shadow of death, I will fear no evil; For You are with me; Your rod and Your staff, they comfort me. You prepare a table before me in the presence of my enemies; You anoint my head with oil; My cup runs over. Surely goodness and mercy shall follow me All the days of my life; And I will dwell in the house of the LORD Forever.

Psalm 23:1-6

Each day, like sheep, we traverse the green pastures of this world. As a people, we would have great difficulty avoiding the wolf- trap troubles of life without Jesus shepherding us. However, God's ways are not our own; He mapped out the destination, route, and pitfalls before we even knew there was a journey. God is our shepherd in that He guides His flock to safety. He leads us into a new and better life in Him, steering us away from the dangers of sin. Today, consider how much you need to surrender in your life to allow God to do what He wants for you, through you, and for His ultimate glory. It is of paramount importance to seek God first and know that He is the reward of life every day. We have the unmerited, undeserved mercy and grace of God in our lives. How He chooses to lead us is entirely up to Him. Our job is to trust Jesus, even if it means walking through valleys and shadows of death.

Lord,
We surrender our lives to You not because we are sure of ourselves or the road ahead, but we are sure of You. Sit on the throne of our hearts that is only meant for You, Jesus. Who You are with us is far more critical than the comforts along the way. Empower us to follow You wherever You lead. Help us to trust You in all we do to Your glory.

Amen.

DAY FOUR:

Where You Go I Go

Entreat me not to leave you, Or to turn back from following after you; For wherever you go, I will go; And wherever you lodge, I will lodge; Your people shall be my people, And your God, my God. Where you die, I will die, and there will I be buried. The LORD do so to me, and more also, If anything but death parts you and me.

Ruth 1:16—17

Have you ever heard the colloquial phrase *ride or die*? It's an endearing term used to describe only the closest of friends or most loyal of allies. In a world where people will leave you in a ditch to save themselves, a relationship like Ruth and Naomi is to be celebrated. For many, trusting or empowering someone comes easier when there is a reciprocal covenant in place. The true test of loyalty, however, is sacrificing for another so that they may thrive. All my life, I have enjoyed such a relationship. Before embarking on our childhood adventures, like Ruth, my sister Sharika and I would often say to each other, "Come on, ride or die!" After her college graduation, Sharika purchased her first car. She planned a road trip from Virginia to Orlando, Florida, and we were off. On our first day at the theme park, we went on all but the last rollercoaster, and then my sister got dizzy! I told her that she didn't have to ride this one, but she finished her water and turned to me, saying, "No: where you go, I go!" Do you have a ride or die friend? If not, try Jesus; He is a friend that will never leave nor forsake you.

Lord,
Help us to be better friends to You and each other. Remind us that loyalty is a valued virtue in Your kingdom. We see Your example in our life as You remain by our side always. You died on the cross for our sins and triumphed. We look up to You and will follow You wherever You lead us. You hold the map while we carry the bags. Riding along for the journey is our most incredible honor. We wouldn't have it any other way.

Amen.

DAY FIVE:

Believe in Him

…Then He brought him outside and said, "Look now toward heaven, and count the stars
if you are able to number them." And He said to him, "So shall your descendants be."
And he believed in the LORD, and He accounted it to him for righteousness.

Genesis 15:5–6

In your life, you are going to hear voices. You find the kind of voices in society telling you what you should be and what you can never be. The voices of people who want the best for you but don't believe you know what your destiny is. The voices within yourself that tell you that you will never attain them because you don't have results in your hands right now. Then there is the still, small voice of God that tells you precisely what you are afraid to believe. He tells you that you can and will. That if you would only stand and believe, He will take care of the rest. Abraham looked at the stars above, not counting how many there were in the sky yet believing God's promise for his family. We, as believers in Christ, are the descendants of Abraham. We are the adopted children of faith. You, too, can look up to those same stars and not know the possibilities that open up to us because we believe God. It's in our blood. Jesus's blood covers our lives and everything that we dare to have faith about. Just like that. There doesn't need to be some existential crisis, some wrestling point, some great sign. It all comes down to a straightforward question: Do you *believe in Him?*

Lord,
Let our relationship with You be one founded on faith. When You
say something about our life, help us to believe You. So many times,
we allow circumstances to cloud the vision of hope You bring into
our lives. Help us to believe and be counted as righteous for that
faith. No doubt. No second-guessing. We believe in You. You are the
same God, yesterday, today, and tomorrow; never let us forget that.

Amen.

PART TWO:
Your Part, His Plan

The steps of a good man are ordered by the Lord, And He delights in his way.

Psalm 37:23

DAY SIX:

Yes, You!

…Then he said, "There remains yet the youngest, and there he is, keeping the sheep." And Samuel said to Jesse, "Send and bring him. For we will not sit down till he comes here." So he sent and brought him in. Now he was ruddy, with bright eyes, and good-looking. And the LORD said, "Arise, anoint him; for this is the one!" Then Samuel took the horn of oil and anointed him in the midst of his brothers; and the Spirit of the LORD came upon David from that day forward. So Samuel arose and went to Ramah.

1 Samuel 16:11–13

David's family thought so little of him that he wasn't invited to meet the prophet, Samuel. David was left tending sheep while his brothers were assembled. In a dismissive tone, Jesse tells the prophet, "There remains yet the youngest, and there he is, keeping the sheep." Led by God, Samuel would not begin until David was invited to join. Isn't it wonderful that although the world may deem you less than, God says you're the one? Why does God label you as the one? Like David, God doesn't choose us because we have a clean heart and a right spirit. The truth is, none of us are perfect… and neither was David. Instead, He chooses us because we trust that He will supply all our needs: "The Lord is my Shepherd; I shall not want" (Psalm 23:1). He chooses us because we seek to spend time with Him: "He makes me lie down in green pastures, He leads me beside still waters" (Psalm 23:2). We are chosen because we know that without God, we are nothing. We realize that our purpose is to bring Glory to Him: "He leads me in the path of righteousness for His name's sake" (Psalm 23:3). It's your humility, not your perfection, that will mark you for God's purpose. He coaches and molds society's underdogs into champions, leaving the world mystified. In a crowd of capable people, God saw your integrity and exclaimed, "This is the one!"

Lord,

When we step into the anointing, You have given us, help us to remember that the outward appearance means next to nothing to You. Let our hearts be acceptable in Your sight so that we may walk in favor, honor, and righteousness before You. Remind us that nothing we do from the point of being chosen by You to the crown You place on our heads happens without you. You know us when we aren't seen. You choose us when it's your time.

Amen.

DAY SEVEN:

You Are Valuable

And when she has found it, she calls her friends and neighbors together, saying, "Rejoice with me, for I have found the piece which I lost!" Likewise, I say to you, there is joy in the presence of the angels of God over one sinner who repents.

Luke 15:9-10

God does not waste His time looking for someone who doesn't matter. Jesus didn't conquer death for you to blend in with the wallpaper. You are very valuable. It doesn't matter what people have told you, what you have said yourself, or what circumstances you have encountered. God still loves you. So much so that He humbled Himself on earth, knowing that you would doubt your worth. The Lord is a God of intention, knowing your weaknesses, crafting your strengths, and calling you back to Him. He doesn't waste His time. He doesn't create us to sit and watch Netflix all day, drinking and partying during the weekends to forget the week's pain. Instead of wasting one of the most valuable things in the universe, put it to use. Pray to God in heaven to hone your life so that you may use it properly. Are you walking with the class and dignity of a child of God? No? If no one has told you yet, let it be my privilege to say *you are valued*. You are better than the sins you get lost in. You are better than your past. When you repent and return to God, He will tell the angels in heaven, "Rejoice with me, for I have found the piece which I lost!"

Lord,
We always want to be found by You. Help us to know that we can turn to You even when we go astray. We need a shepherd to see us and someone to sweep the house for us. You are the only one who can pick us up and take us to where we need to be. Lord, please help us believe in who You created us to be. Father, You are more valuable than we are. Help us to strive to be more like Your son Jesus.

Amen.

DAY EIGHT:

A New Start

Then the dove came to him in the evening, and behold, a freshly plucked olive leaf was in her mouth; and Noah knew that the waters had receded from the earth. So, he waited yet another seven days and sent out the dove, which did not return again to him anymore.

Genesis 8:11–12

A new start is never easy. Having endured the great flood and the months of waiting for the waters to abate, Noah, after receiving the olive leaf, waited another seven days before sending the dove out again. He didn't know when the waters would dry enough to leave the ark. He only knew that they would… because God said they would. Do you have enough patience to wait on the Lord to tell you when to get your promise? Noah began his new life by doing what was in his control and trusting in God. Your new life doesn't depend on conditions being just right by your standards; they must be right by His standard. You might not know how things will turn out or when, but you can be confident they will. The unchanging truth of God's word is the mountain upon which your ark can land. Then after the storms in your life are over, you can rejoice like Noah, praising God for who He is and what He has done in your life. Go through the flood, my friend, and accept the new start God has planned for you!

Lord,
Our prayers are sent out to you, hoping to coincide with what You desire for us. We need Your help to grow patience for our deliverance and be aware that you are working even if the change is not yet complete. God, encourage us with Your presence. Guide us in Your word. Relieve any stress we have by giving us the wisdom to build even when it is difficult.

Amen.

DAY NINE:

It's Bigger Than You

...Do not think in your heart that you will escape in the king's palace any more than all the other Jews. For if you remain completely silent at this time, relief and deliverance will arise for the Jews from another place, but you and your father's house will perish. Yet who knows whether you have come to the kingdom for such a time as this?

Esther 4:13–14

There comes a time in everyone's life when they must choose to focus only on themselves or make an impact. Either you will blend into the background or stand up for what you believe in. When you see the pains, struggles, and sorrows of the world, yet you do nothing, you are complicit. As believers in Christ, we have an answer to all problems: His name is Jesus! Those addicted to drugs can change their life with the support of a believing community around them. Victims of abuse may see their worth if we see worth in them. Providing food and shelter for the homeless are tangible ways to make an impact. By being who we say we are, we can be precisely what the world needs us to be. The first step is realizing that Jesus's mission *is more significant than you!* If you don't choose to help, relief and deliverance will arise for God's people from another place.

Lord,
Don't let us get so complacent in our way of life that we don't receive Your will. Help us to be brave even in harsher situations if need be. Give us the inner resolve to place ourselves in front and stand for what we believe. Don't let us shrink back and pretend to be something we aren't. Grow us so that we can help others.

Amen.

DAY TEN:

A Perfect Plan with Imperfect Pieces

…Do not be afraid, for am I in the place of God? But as for you, you meant evil against me; but God meant it for good, in order to bring it about as it is this day, to save many people alive.

Genesis 50:19–20

Have you ever sat down to finish a puzzle? Some pieces fit nicely, like the edges; it can take us a crazy amount of time to find others' proper place. The puzzle may take minutes, hours, or even days, depending on the number of pieces and the artwork's caliber when assembled. If the art is the only fruit in a basket, it will be simple. If it is a mountain house by the river, in the snow, you might as well get comfortable for the next couple of days. As imperfect people in the puzzle of life, there are times when our plans don't fit nicely in the mold God has created for our lives. He has designed, cut, and shaped us: we just have to trust His plan. Joseph was his father's favorite son. This made his brothers fear that he would possibly rule over them one day. When Joseph became boastful about his dreams and beautiful cloak, they sold him into slavery. He learned an important lesson about humility, so when his brothers came to him in need, he helped them. Joseph and his brothers were all *imperfect pieces in God's perfect plan.* You don't have to be perfect for God to use you… you only have to be willing!

Lord,
When you created us, You knew that we couldn't achieve greatness by ourselves. Allow us to feel the grace You shed onto our lives today as we move forward in faith. Even if we see more parts of our story with pain, You know the ultimate plan. Use all of our life for Your glory, Jesus. Enable us always to believe that.

Amen.

DAY ELEVEN:

God Has the Long Game

So Mephibosheth dwelt in Jerusalem, for he ate continually at the king's table.
And he was lame in both his feet.

2 Samuel 9:13

No one understood why David forgave his enemy's family. No one could have envisioned the blessing that the king would bestow upon the disabled young man; no one except God. God, in His infinite wisdom, sees all people, their hearts, and their desires. When God chose David to be king, He did so knowing that there would be jealousy and mistrust along the way. When God calls you, it doesn't matter if you are lame, addicted, maltreated, or slow of tongue. He will take your weaknesses and use them for your good. He will calculate your adversary's moves against you, ensuring a victory. You may make terrible decisions on your journey—there may be times when you won't move at all— but you will never walk alone. The fact that Mephibosheth was lame didn't prohibit his blessing, and neither did anyone's protest. If David could do that for an enemy, *God's long game* will certainly do that for you, His child.

Lord,
Remind us that even though we don't see why every heartbreak, mistake, trial, or burden occurs in our life, You are still the king of order. You are right on time, Jesus, and we await Your call on our experience. Progression in the soul is always worth the wait. When we are broken, let us still hear Your call to redeem us. Thank You, Lord!

Amen.

DAY TWELVE:

Trust and Believe

When she heard about Jesus, she came behind Him in the crowd and touched
His garment. For she said, "If only I may touch His clothes, I shall be made well."
Immediately the fountain of her blood was dried up, and she felt in her body
that she was healed of the affliction.

Mark 5:27–29

In the scripture above, we read about a woman making her way to Jesus through a crowd. Everyone else was walking around Jesus, but this woman boldly dared to touch Him. Encumbered with an issue of blood, she risked her life for a blessing. Her faith was strong enough to capture the attention of God; a faith forged by desperation. Although the circumstances seem simple on the surface, she dared to *trust and believe* God would heal her if only she could touch the hem of His garments. So many of us think that we need to be perfect for God to hear our prayers or that we need to be mature Christians. In reality, God acknowledges those who touch Him, trusting not in what they think may happen but accepting the truth of who He is. This woman had plain to see issues, and her faith produced evidence of things she hoped for. She overrode her fears and social stigma because she decided to reach Jesus was worth any risk. God does the work… Our only job is to trust and believe!

Lord,
Please come into our hearts and let us acknowledge that, with-
out trusting You, we cannot indeed have a relationship with You.
Although You came to us to fulfill the law and relieve us of the bur-
den of sin, You did require something of us: faith. While we seem
to be surrounded by unbelief, let us be daring enough to call upon
Your name. Remember us God. Don't leave us without changing us
according to Your will.

Amen.

DAY THIRTEEN:

Focus

…And they awoke Him and said to Him, "Teacher, do You not care that we are perishing?" Then He arose and rebuked the wind, and said to the sea, "Peace, be still!" And the wind ceased and there was a great calm. But He said to them, "Why are you so fearful? How is it that you have no faith?" And they feared exceedingly, and said to one another, "Who can this be, that even the wind and the sea obey Him!"

Mark 4:38-41

Inside, your emotions swell as the circumstances of life twist and turn around you. The worse the storm in your life gets, the more aware you are of your frailty. You ask God "How do you expect me to do the impossible?" but you forget who is in the boat with you. Whenever God speaks, the world takes notice. His presence and will are undeniable. When Jesus picks you to get into a boat and says, "Follow me," nothing else matters. You heard Him. You believe Him. You know Him – chase after God full speed ahead. In our scripture, the disciples get caught up like so many of us with details that don't matter. We stop and think, "Can't you see what is happening to me? My life isn't supposed to be like this!" Yet the beautiful truth about Jesus is that He reorients your focus back onto Him if you are willing to trust Him in the storm. We must accept His challenge for us to dig in, setting our feet on the rock of our salvation. Choosing to look at Jesus today during our trials, we know that He's the only one that matters. No matter how rough life gets, He's worth going through any storm for. Stay focused.

Lord,
Please empower us to keep walking in the path You set for us despite the onslaught of distractions in our way. Lest we forget how we came to You in the first place, let us hold on to You and focus on all the truth, wisdom, and love You have shown us in our life. Give us the strength to reach out to You, even if we feel like we are sinking from time to time.

Amen.

DAY FOURTEEN:

Less of You, More of God

And the Lord said to Gideon, "The people who are with you are too many for Me to give the Midianites into their hands, lest Israel claim glory for itself against Me, saying, 'My own hand has saved me.' Now therefore, proclaim in the hearing of the people, saying, 'Whoever is fearful and afraid, let him turn and depart at once from Mount Gilead.'" And twenty-two thousand of the people returned, and ten thousand remained.

Judges 7:2–3

Our scripture today finds Gideon well aware of his shortcomings. He is the smallest member of the weakest clan in Israel, yet God calls him to do what seems impossible on the outside. Gideon takes soldiers to fight the battle, but God, in His signature twist, says there are "too many" people. Often when we win a battle in our life, we color the past to enhance our image, remembering the facts differently. As adults, we tend to say "I got here myself. *I* thought of moving here. *I* took the opportunity. *I* studied, and *I* passed. *I* earned my promotion!" All the while, knowing deep down that we got on our knees and prayed for results. While God rarely receives credit when it is due, He, sometimes, makes it clear and without a doubt who is working for whom. A decisive victory against all *human* capability and logic. Only God thinks of every detail and achieves perfection as He does. When He willingly supplies our needs, we should willingly acknowledge Him first. It doesn't matter how strong we think we are; we are nothing without God. It's time to be kingdom-minded instead of self-minded; this means less of you and more of God.

Lord,
Allow us to listen closely to what you want us to do and remember. You were the one who led us here. It's not about what accomplishments we believe we have achieved or what accolades we acquire but the God we serve. Remind us what a privilege it is to serve You and honor You with everything we have. Don't let us hold back from falling in love with You more and our self-image less.

Amen.

DAY FIFTEEN:

Ordered Steps

The steps of a good man are ordered by the LORD, And He delights in his way.
Though he fall, he shall not be utterly cast down; For the LORD upholds him with His
hand. I have been young, and now am old; Yet I have not seen the righteous forsaken,
Nor his descendants begging for bread.

Psalm 37:23-25

I remember going to my grandmother's church in Alabama. The congregation would often sing to the good Lord above, saying, *lead me, guide me along the Way!* (anonymous/traditional hymn). They knew that God in His infinite wisdom, holiness, and righteousness does not think like us. As the creator of all things, He didn't throw us into life without considering the details. Our Father has a plan for our lives. Tucked within His plan of redemption is a divine order for the steps of the good and righteous. Everything in the universe benefits from God's love and His grace. If God takes care of the stars in the sky, the plants, and the animals, He will certainly do so for His blood-bought children. When you walk in God's plan, do His will in His way… He will be delighted, and you will never be forsaken.

Lord,
Help us to see our lives as you do. You are the only one who loves
us while genuinely knowing us. We read in your word that you have
plans to prosper us and not harm us. Let us grab hold of you and
believe that. Remind us that even if we were to fall one day, you are
faithful to pick us back up. Encourage us to walk without all the
details, trusting you with the map to our lives.

Amen.

PART THREE:
Journey with Christ

For God has not given us a spirit of fear,
but of power and of love and of a sound mind.

2 Timothy 1:7

DAY SIXTEEN:

Counting the Cost

Now Jesus sat opposite the treasury and saw how the people put money into the treasury. And many who were rich put in much. Then one poor widow came and threw in two mites, which make a quadrans. So He called His disciples to Himself and said to them, "Assuredly, I say to you that this poor widow has put in more than all those who have given to the treasury; for they all put in out of their abundance, but she out of her poverty put in all that she had, her whole livelihood."

Mark 12:41-44

The world tends to value material achievements above all else. Most wealthy people will give but only to the extent which they deem worthy. Today's affluent are often lauded for their vast wealth, luxury cars, expansive homes, and the latest technological devices. However, this was not so with Jesus. He was not impressed with those who gave out of their abundance; what made Jesus stop and take note was the woman who scrounged up everything she had and gave it to God. Ultimately, everything we possess has come from God, and when we give our very best, it impacts our relationship with Him. The price you are willing to pay for something indicates the value you place on it. Before speaking us into existence, God knew the price he would have to pay for our salvation. He never stopped to count the cost. He simply gave all He had— His whole livelihood! How much will you deliver?

Lord,
Let us find value in what You value! Allow us to encourage one another to give our all to You, even when the world doesn't do the same. Work in us so that we may have joy in loving You, above all else. Renew our minds so that we can have the wisdom to give more than we receive in life.

Amen.

DAY SEVENTEEN:

Waiting on Jesus

For an angel went down at a certain time into the pool and stirred up the water; then whoever stepped in first, after the stirring of the water, was made well of whatever disease he had. Now a certain man was there who had an infirmity thirty-eight years. When Jesus saw him lying there, and knew that he already had been in that condition a long time, He said to him, "Do you want to be made well?" The sick man answered Him, "Sir, I have no man to put me into the pool when the water is stirred up; but while I am coming, another steps down before me." Jesus said to him, "Rise, take up your bed and walk." And immediately the man was made well, took up his bed, and walked. And that day was the Sabbath.

John 5:4–9

When I was sixteen years old, I experienced a horrible knee injury. Afterward, I walked around in baggy sweatpants to hide the giant brace supporting my leg and to mask the limp in my gait. I was effectively disabled for that year, and the unrelenting questioning I received made it all the more painful. Let us consider how this man felt so close to healing but never getting it for thirty-eight years. Everyone else would beat him to the water because he was simply unable to move fast enough. No one helped him because, in the culture of the day, he was supposed to help himself. When Jesus acknowledged the man before fixing the situation, he not only healed his body but his broken spirit as well. After *thirty-eight years of waiting*, he was given an opportunity that some of us aren't willing to wait two days for. So much life can happen between now and your breakthrough, but that doesn't mean that it will never happen. After a year and a half, I had yet another surgery, and now I'm walking tall with no limp. I've learned to *wait on Jesus*.

Lord,
In the midst of our waiting for a breakthrough, let us remember that You never fail. Don't let us think of reasons to stay put when you tell us to get up and walk. Don't let us get comfortable staying in our past hurts and traumas. Remind us that our present challenges are nothing compared to what You will do in our lives.

Amen.

DAY EIGHTEEN:

Don't Give Him Up

He said to him the third time, "Simon, son of Jonah, do you love Me?" Peter was grieved because He said to him the third time, "Do you love Me?" And he said to Him, "Lord, You know all things; You know that I love You." Jesus said to him, "Feed My sheep. Most assuredly, I say to you, when you were younger, you girded yourself and walked where you wished; but when you are old, you will stretch out your hands, and another will gird you and carry you where you do not wish."

John 21:17–18

In today's scripture, Peter has realized that Jesus was right about his character. When pressed and when faith was no longer popular, Peter gave Jesus up three times. It wasn't that Peter was a bad man, but he was a man riddled with the fear of death. So many of us puff ourselves up as great Christians, all the while not reconciling our sinful selves to God. We don't want to believe that we can still do wrong even after knowing Jesus for so long. Christians can have difficulty admitting their faith in media or at work, school, or home, especially in dire circumstances. The truth is the road is not always pretty, and people get hurt, die, or even get locked up for their faith. Yet, at the end of the day, you must decide if Jesus is worth losing everything. Jesus will invite us back if we are willing to change, but *don't ever give Him up once you come back.* Run this good race of faith until the sweet or even bitter end. Three times, Peter was given the question by Jesus: *Do you love me?* Each time that Peter said yes, Jesus told him to feed His sheep. When we mess up, the best way to move forward is to get back to work, serving God's people in love and truth.

Lord,
When the pressures of the world and the tensions within our hearts become too much for us to handle, empower us to never give up on what you called us to be. Jesus, our relationship with You is more important than our ego and what people think of us. Give us the strength to not cower behind excuses but to stand with You willingly all of our life.

Amen.

DAY NINETEEN:

Don't Doubt-Check

Then she sent and called for Barak the son of Abinoam from Kedesh in Naphtali, and said to him, "Has not the LORD God of Israel commanded, 'Go and deploy troops at Mount Tabor; take with you ten thousand men of the sons of Naphtali and of the sons of Zebulun; and against you I will deploy Sisera, the commander of Jabin's army, with his chariots and his multitude at the River Kishon; and I will deliver him into your hand'?" And Barak said to her, "If you will go with me, then I will go; but if you will not go with me, I will not go!" So she said, "I will surely go with you; nevertheless there will be no glory for you in the journey you are taking, for the LORD will sell Sisera into the hand of a woman." Then Deborah arose and went with Barak to Kedesh.

Judges 4:6–9

Here, Israel's warriors have been called to go into battle, but their commander is terrified of leading. He tells the prophetess, "If you will go with me, then I will go; but if you will not go with me, I will not go!" (Judges 4:8) as if she didn't just tell him what God told them to do. We often think that if God doesn't tell us twenty times or show us a miracle, then He isn't with us. When God calls you into service, He never fails to provide backup. Through many sleepless nights, we toss and turn in our beds wondering, *Will I be successful?* The truth is, we strategize to be our best selves in the future, losing the beauty of right now. Right now, you can step into the call that Jesus has on your life. Nothing can disqualify you from it, except your willingness to take hold of it. Distractions will come, mistakes will be made, but earnestly striving to do the will of God ensures success. The King of Kings always follows through, and *doubt-checking* Him is an insult.

Lord,
Here we are asking You to help our unbelief. No matter what we encounter in this life, let us have such anointed faith that it transforms our relationship with You. Let our lives reflect an undaunted and unflinching faith in You, so that whoever looks on our lives will be inspired.
Amen.

DAY TWENTY:

Love Overcomes Loss

And they remembered His words. Then they returned from the tomb and told all these things to the eleven and to all the rest. It was Mary Magdalene, Joanna, Mary the mother of James, and the other women with them, who told these things to the apostles. And their words seemed to them like idle tales, and they did not believe them. But Peter arose and ran to the tomb; and stooping down, he saw the linen cloths lying by themselves; and he departed, marveling to himself at what had happened.

Luke 24:8–12

As you grow up, you learn that you understand life backward yet live forward. We don't have all the pieces, and we can't know the full future or the reasons why things happen. We are terrified of loss because it is inevitable. There may be moments in our lives when we will see the death of something we've cherished. A career, a relationship, self-image, or dreams may go in the blink of an eye. As a result, we're left bewildered, wondering how what we believed in and loved can be gone. We look to the graves of our lives and wonder where do we go from here. It is then that we remember that the love of God is capable of *overcoming every loss*. Jesus got back up again, defeating death, hell, and the grave. The changes that we need for our life depends on Jesus, and He already got up for us. We must decide that life and love are worth fighting for and that loss doesn't define us... but our belief and love for Jesus do.

Lord,
Please create the right spirit throughout our day, our tumultuous emotions, and unexpected circumstances so that we can hold on for the change You bring. Let us remember that the same power that resurrected Your son Jesus from the grave is within us. Give us the faith to get up and out of what is expected; help us rise to the occasion of what You want us to do.

Amen.

DAY TWENTY-ONE:

Press On

Not that I have already attained, or am already perfected; but I press on, that I may lay hold of that for which Christ Jesus has also laid hold of me. Brethren, I do not count myself to have apprehended; but one thing I do, forgetting those things which are behind and reaching forward to those things which are ahead, I press toward the goal for the prize of the upward call of God in Christ Jesus. Therefore let us, as many as are mature, have this mind; and if in anything you think otherwise, God will reveal even this to you. Nevertheless, to the degree that we have already attained, let us walk by the same rule, let us be of the same mind.

Philippians 3:12–16

At the beginning of our journey with Christ, we realized we would never be the same. He touched our hearts when it was desperate and calling out for Him. He then revealed Himself, and His glory enthralls us. We realize that while we may not receive every desire of our hearts… that He will supply all our needs, good people will suffer, and Christians will still make mistakes. In the passage shared today, we come to terms with our current state as believers in progress. The moment we believed in Jesus, we were saved; every day afterward is a process called sanctification. It becomes irrevocably clear that we never deserved God's sacrifice nor blessings and that being alive right now is a gift. As maturing Christians, we strive to be more and more like Jesus. Even through pain, depression, heartache, disappointment, separation, and discomfort, we press forward to grasp what God has promised. God is real, true to His Word, and He is in control, and thus, we shouldn't think of Him in simplistic human ways. He is not a formula of a prayer or a tithe; He is God. As a Christian, your body, actions, and future are planned according to His purpose. You may not have everything together presently, but you must *press on* toward the goal for the prize of the upward call of God!

Lord,

None of us have achieved all that You have asked. We all have so much to do. But if You could help us believe, trust, and hope in You more, we can make it. Turn our lives around, Lord. Let us be better, not because we are perfect in ourselves but because we believe that you have already done it all.

Amen.

PART FOUR:

Get Ready to Fight

Fight the good fight of faith, lay hold on eternal life,
to which you were also called and have confessed the good confession
in the presence of many witnesses.

1 Timothy 6:12

DAY TWENTY-TWO:

A New Life Not Old Mess

Jesus said to her, "Woman, believe Me, the hour is coming when you will neither on this mountain, nor in Jerusalem, worship the Father. You worship what you do not know; we know what we worship, for salvation is of the Jews. But the hour is coming, and now is, when the true worshipers will worship the Father in spirit and truth; for the Father is seeking such to worship Him. God is Spirit, and those who worship Him must worship in spirit and truth."

The woman said to Him, "I know that Messiah is coming" (who is called Christ). "When He comes, He will tell us all things." Jesus said to her, "I who speak to you am He."

John 4:21–26

The woman from Samaria was shocked that Jesus was speaking with her at all. The deep ethnic division between Jews and Gentiles seemed impossible to overcome. However, Jesus was not concerned with the woman's ethnicity. He wanted people to truly worship Him in spirit and in truth. He chose this woman to spread the gospel to those who did not know Him; a woman with a past and different ethnicity. Many Christians take God for granted. They mistakenly believe that being saved means they can continue to sin without any consequence. But Jesus didn't die on the cross for us to have unlimited opportunities to sin. Accepting salvation means making a turn away from your sins. There may be times when you will be tired of the life you are living. This could be either from your choices or the situations you have been through. Yet the love of Jesus, with the renewed mind, heart, and actions brought by the Holy Spirit, is more than enough to revitalize and stabilize you. It doesn't matter that you have a past. It doesn't matter that your present is tough. What matters is that the God you serve is always with you, and if you are willing, He will give you what matters. A *new life* worth living… but only if you leave the *old mess* behind.

Lord,

Please revive us with a fresh filling of Your Holy Spirit. Let us remember who is within us and what You have done for us always. Never let us get so complacent that we settle for junk instead of the promises You have given us. Tell us where we go wrong, and empower us to follow You, while giving us the wisdom and the courage to love You.

Amen.

DAY TWENTY-THREE:

It's Already Done

But as God is faithful, our word to you was not Yes and No. For the Son of God, Jesus Christ, who was preached among you by us—by me, Silvanus, and Timothy—was not Yes and No, but in Him was Yes. For all the promises of God in Him are Yes, and in Him Amen, to the glory of God through us. Now He who establishes us with you in Christ and has anointed us is God, who also has sealed us and given us the Spirit in our hearts as a guarantee.

2 Corinthians 1:18–22

Your faith has made an appointment with God, and now your destiny is secure. Before laying the foundation of the world, God set you apart. He wrote the story, set the scene, and said yes to blessing you. Believing allowed you to step onto the set of God's promises. When you claimed Jesus, your guaranteed yes was secured. Your value now is placed on who you are, not what you've done. We can fail a thousand times in the eyes of a crowd, but the only yeses that matter are the ones from God. Are you willing to take that vote of confidence? The God of everything believes in you. Yes, you will have struggles and pain, but they're only preparation for more remarkable things He has in store for you. Walk through the adversity, and you will receive God's guarantee. Your destiny is a yes, sitting on God's shelf, waiting for you. *It's already done!*

Father in heaven,
We honor you above all else. Lord, we thank you for choosing us before the foundation of the very world. No matter who or what we are, we know one thing for sure: you, God, are supreme. You didn't have any second thoughts about us; you decided the moment you created. Thank you for being our King and our Father. Whenever we step into a room, allow us to walk in knowing we are children of God.

Amen.

DAY TWENTY-FOUR:

Whatever It Takes

But when Paul had gathered a bundle of sticks and laid them on the fire, a viper came out because of the heat, and fastened on his hand. So when the natives saw the creature hanging from his hand, they said to one another, "No doubt this man is a murderer, whom, though he has escaped the sea, yet justice does not allow to live." But he shook off the creature into the fire and suffered no harm. However, they were expecting that he would swell up or suddenly fall down dead. But after they had looked for a long time and saw no harm come to him, they changed their minds and said that he was a god.

Acts 28:3–6

Paul indeed felt he'd had enough calamity for one trip. His ship sank, he was stranded on an island, and when he at last found some semblance of rest, he got bitten by a poisonous snake. What a day! This didn't deter Paul, though, because he knew deep down inside that God meant for him to go to Rome. No matter how many trials came his way, he knew one thing was for sure: he could not and would not die there. He had too much left to do according to God's will. When you step with God, you know that all the troubles you face are temporary moments in your story. You're never out for the count simply because things get rough on the road. You're done when God says you are done, and as believers, we must be willing to do whatever it takes to arrive at our purpose. There may never be a perfect time or a great feeling to set out on your journey. The determination to do *whatever it takes* and go wherever God leads you will get results regardless of the crowd's opinion.

Father,
You know that even though trouble can be on our journey, that is no indication of whether You are with us. Your plan for us can survive storms. Your decisions for our lives outweigh circumstantial poison and rumors. Father, You have the final say, and no matter what comes our way, let our conviction of Your word guide us.

Amen.

DAY TWENTY-FIVE:

Loss Is Gain

But what things were gain to me, these I have counted loss for Christ. Yet indeed I also count all things loss for the excellence of the knowledge of Christ Jesus my Lord, for whom I have suffered the loss of all things, and count them as rubbish, that I may gain Christ and be found in Him, not having my own righteousness, which is from the law, but that which is through faith in Christ, the righteousness which is from God by faith; that I may know Him and the power of His resurrection, and the fellowship of His sufferings, being conformed to His death, if, by any means, I may attain to the resurrection from the dead.

Philippians 3:7–11

Let us dive into what it feels like to be in the world but not part of it. Paul wrote to the Philippians about the joy of finding Christ in his life. Before his life-changing encounter on the road to Damascus, Paul was revered in Jewish society. He came from the right background, knew the right people, and had all the ins and the education to be truly elite. However, when he met Jesus and was saved… he counted all that background as rubbish. Purely trash in comparison to what he would gain in Christ. Nothing we do is enough to earn our way into heaven. The only merit we have is our faith; no more, no less. One thing that I've always heard is, "You can't take your money to the grave." It doesn't matter your status, how much education you have, or how often you go to church: your soul and the faith you have built within are the only things you can take with you. A life spent serving self… is a life spent poorly. Massive piles of wealth, notoriety, and accolades from other people mean nothing. What did you do with your faith? Did you believe in what mattered? What did you do with that belief? These are the things that define you. If you fill your life with empty things, you will be empty.

Father,

When we realize that who you are is more important than anything, give us the courage to be bold. Increase our strength to walk away from past mistakes and, more importantly, present temptations. Grant us the ability to go all-in on our love for you. Let us place you in your proper superior position in our lives. Everything else isn't worth our time if you aren't involved. Let us be so about your business on the earth that no one and nothing will stop us from expressing it.

Amen.

DAY TWENTY-SIX:

Get Out of Your Feelings

Then God said to Jonah, "Is it right for you to be angry about the plant?" And he said, "It is right for me to be angry, even to death!" But the LORD said, "You have had pity on the plant for which you have not labored, nor made it grow, which came up in a night and perished in a night. And should I not pity Nineveh, that great city, in which are more than one hundred and twenty thousand persons who cannot discern between their right hand and their left—and much livestock?"

Jonah 4:9–11

Suppose you're on a road trip and you need to stop for gas. The closest city is the hometown of someone who has treated you wrong in the past. When you arrive, you look at what surrounds you: different trees, buildings with different architectural designs, and other people. You get out of the car and realize that you don't feel comfortable in the area. Do you treat the people with kindness or with skepticism when you arrive? Today, we look at Jonah and his journey to Nineveh. Although God sent Jonah to the city, he refused because of the bad blood between his people and theirs. When the city repented and turned to God, he was still profoundly unsatisfied with them. Chewing on the bad memories that refused to die in his heart, he always wished for their destruction. God had forgiven Nineveh for their transgressions; Jonah had not. Who was in the wrong? Jonah! He couldn't get past his anguish enough to participate in God's plan. Don't let your prejudices get in the way of witnessing and being a part of a move of God. As Christians, whenever we walk into a room, we serve as ambassadors for the kingdom of God. It may not be a quest you want to be on, but it is your job to step in right now. *Get out of your feelings!* Be happy that more people are coming to Christ, not just the people you think are so-called right.

Father,

Teach us how to get past our prejudices and emotions to see the bigger picture. Use us to reach others. Teach us how to love past boundaries and comforts so that we can be more like You, Jesus. Let our love for others outweigh any little insights we might have. Show us the way, Lord.

Amen.

DAY TWENTY-SEVEN:

Spiritual Fight

If you do well, will you not be accepted? And if you do not do well, sin lies at the door. And its desire is for you, but you should rule over it.

Genesis 4:7

As a Tae Kwon Do athlete, I loved to compete in tournaments. I was a ten-time national champion, and sparring (fighting) was my specialty. It wasn't often that I would lose a fight, and with every round, my goal was to give it my all. As glorious as the feeling of winning was, nothing was as crushing as defeat. In our scripture today, Cain is acting as if he has already lost the spiritual fight of his life. God seeing Cain sulking after losing to his brother, tries to let Cain know ahead of time what he is in for. A coach will tell a fighter which techniques to use and to avoid typical mistakes. God tells us to keep our eyes on Him, our hands up in prayer, and our mind on what He has called us to do. On the outside, Cain's anger or bitterness looks like something anyone would do, but instead of listening to God, he lets his one-time loss become a lifetime of defeat. In life, we all have problems and sin, but the day we let our shame get in the way of repenting and embracing God is when we are truly defeated. Your spiritual fight is not over. Get back up, and keep on praying, fasting, and loving God.

Father,
As we pray today, let us not be ashamed of our losses. You give us the courage to get back up and fight another round. All of creation awaits You, and we who have Your Holy Spirit groan every day waiting for You. We want to experience that ultimate win with You, but give us the courage to move at this moment right now.

Amen.

DAY TWENTY-EIGHT:

Same Fight Different Opponent

Moreover, David said, "The LORD, who delivered me from the paw of the lion and from the paw of the bear, He will deliver me from the hand of this Philistine." And Saul said to David, "Go, and the LORD be with you!"

1 Samuel 17:37

Before David fights Goliath, he recounts all the other brushes with death that God saved him from. No matter how fierce, a giant man is no scarier than a lion or bear running straight at you: it's the *same fight... different opponent*. David's earlier experience was valuable not only because he knew his fighting skills, but previous successes made him braver in faith. If you've already fought a more significant battle, all the others pale in comparison. God allows us to go through specific difficulties to be more equipped for the kinds of struggles that He wants us to face. As Christians, we learn that conflicts are inevitable; we just have to be well prepared before they begin. It doesn't matter what opponent you face today; you are well prepared for the challenge with God.

Lord,
You have already won it all. Every battle scar we have has shown us how merciful and gracious You are. Enlarge our territory, God, as we embrace our fight. Never let us forget that regardless of how big our problem may seem, it is just another opponent about to go down.

Amen.

DAY TWENTY-NINE:

Help in Unexpected Ways

A certain woman of the wives of the sons of the prophets cried out to Elisha, saying,
"Your servant my husband is dead, and you know that your servant feared the LORD.
And the creditor is coming to take my two sons to be his slaves."

So Elisha said to her, "What shall I do for you? Tell me, what do you have in the house?"
And she said, "Your maidservant has nothing in the house but a jar of oil." Then he
said, "Go, borrow vessels from everywhere, from all your neighbors—empty vessels; do not
gather just a few. And when you have come in, you shall shut the door behind you and your
sons; then pour it into all those vessels, and set aside the full ones."

2 Kings 4:1–4

Today we find a woman with nothing but debt from her husband's death. Everything she once valued is on the line, and so she turns to God for a solution. As we look at our own lives, we cannot fathom what God will do if we only trust and believe in Him. Remembering that the unlimited God we serve is always with us should bring us tremendous joy and peace. My grandma is a living testimony of this. When I was young, she and I would have great conversations concerning the seemingly impossible task of raising seven children. Always her response was a hearty laugh, and then she would say, "God supplies all our needs. He provides *help in unexpected ways!*" Directing her path, God would point her to what she already had to fill the gaps in her life. She used her seamstress abilities to bring extra income into the home. Each summer, she planted a garden and canned fruits and vegetables in preparation for the long winters. She said that it was God who'd blessed her with these gifts. We must praise, trust, and love God, while He does His work by providing all our needs. You should never think you won't make it. The question is not *if* but *how* God is going to pull you through this time.

Father,

Difficult times allow us to look deeper into who we are. You are the God that provides everything, but most importantly, you are the provision. Please don't let us overlook you or any answers you have provided beforehand. Our trust, our help, our lives are in your hands. The best place to be is right where you are.

Amen.

PART FIVE:

Do It Anyway

*He who has My commandments and keeps them, it is he who loves Me.
And he who loves Me will be loved by My Father, and I will love him
and manifest Myself to him.*

John 14:21

DAY THIRTY:

Unexpected Orders

Then Ananias answered, "Lord, I have heard from many about this man, how much harm he has done to Your saints in Jerusalem. And here he has authority from the chief priests to bind all who call on Your name." But the Lord said to him, "Go, for he is a chosen vessel of Mine to bear My name before Gentiles, kings, and the children of Israel. For I will show him how many things he must suffer for My name's sake."

Acts 9:13–16

The one thing we can't stop is the hand of God on a situation. No one thought it would be Saul, the Christian killer, who would spread the gospel. No one wanted to touch Saul, much less bless him. Ananias would reluctantly be the one chosen to carry out that task. There are times when what God asks shakes us to our core. When He surprises us, it reminds us that He is God. We should never put God in a box of our limited understanding. If a simple change of direction deters you, then you need to check yourself. Are you relying on the rock of who God is or on the sand of the things you think He should be? Ananias obeying God at that moment blessed much of the world by answering an unexpected call with complete surrender. When God said to stop protesting and handle the matter, Ananias did just that. Trusting God even when you receive *unexpected orders* is a privilege. It should excite you to take on new challenges because that means new glory for God will be on the other side. Every day there's new marching orders; each day is also filled with new mercies. What you do in a moment of obedience is worth more than a lifetime of prudence.

God,
Don't let us hesitate to follow Your direction. Whoever and what-ever You have planned, let us be willing to go and do the task at hand. Our fears have no place here. Unforgiveness has no place here. We need Your word now. We are ready to move. We are ready to change. At your command, we move; we don't need to under-stand immediately. We just say, "Yes, Lord!"
Amen.

DAY THIRTY-ONE:

Believing without Seeing

So they again called the man who was blind, and said to him, "Give God the glory! We know that this Man is a sinner." He answered and said, "Whether He is a sinner or not I do not know. One thing I know: that though I was blind, now I see." Then they said to him again, "What did He do to you? How did He open your eyes?" He answered them, "I told you already, and you did not listen. Why do you want to hear it again? Do you also want to become His disciples?"

John 9:24–27

There will be times in your life when you absolutely cannot explain what God did. It will just happen. God will step in and do what He does best just because He can. In today's scripture, we see a man who was born blind and who came across Jesus. After his healing, he is questioned about where Jesus went and who He was. The only thing the blind man can attest to was the change he felt in his own life: "One thing I know: that though I was blind, now I see"(verse 25). You may be asked by friends, coworkers, or even your family members about how you know Jesus is the Savior of the world. They may not want to hear your testimony; however, the changes God has made in your life will be unavoidable. *Believing without seeing* is evidence of our faith. We can't know the plan of God, but we know He is working. We don't know precisely how prayer works, but we know that God hears us. As Christians, our testimonies can light the path to God, and our visible righteousness can inspire others to journey toward Him.

Father,
Give us the strength to believe for the rest of our lives for your goodness to take root in our hearts. God, let our testimony of who you are ring out, so that whoever witnesses our praise will have to stop and ask, "Who is Jesus?" What an honor! All glory to you, God!

Amen.

DAY THIRTY-TWO:

Resolve

Again, the devil took Him up on an exceedingly high mountain, and showed Him all the kingdoms of the world and their glory. And he said to Him, "All these things I will give You if You will fall down and worship me." Then Jesus said to him, "Away with you, Satan! For it is written, 'You shall worship the LORD your God, and Him only you shall serve.'" Then the devil left Him, and behold, angels came and ministered to Him.

Matthew 4:8–11

Imagine walking into a classroom full of rowdy children. The instructions you were given are to observe and not interfere with the class. Standing tall above the children, they swarm your ankles. They poke you and say, "You can't do it with your fat head!" or "Only a teacher can solve this one" or "You couldn't even finish your last task." As an adult with an objective, you don't participate or even acknowledge them. You know what is at stake. A thought crosses your mind throughout the chaos: *"I have nothing to prove to a bunch of kids. Stay on mission."* Then only minutes away from completing your task, a boy leaps across the room to hit your arm, hard. What if I told you that being a Christian in the world is similar? That every time you decide to make the right choice or do the right thing, you will face opposition? You will encounter people who dislike you, difficult situations, and dwindling *resolve*. Jesus decided to place His love for God, above all else, even Himself. It didn't matter if the adversary offered riches, scoffed, or preyed on Jesus's weakness: Jesus never faulted. In the middle of our trials, we, too, must always remember who God is. Our love for God should outweigh our discomfort and supersede self-interest.

Father,
When we come to your throne, we want to hear, "Well done, good and faithful servant (Matthew 25:23)." We want to endure past the threats, demands, distractions, and temptations of the devil. God, empower us to be satisfied in our lives for you. It is better to be poor with you than rich without you. It is better to have you near us than to be forever out of your grace.

Amen.

DAY THIRTY-THREE:

Not Enough

*Then Jesus said, "Make the people sit down." Now there was much grass in the place.
So the men sat down, in number about five thousand. And Jesus took the loaves, and when
He had given thanks He distributed them to the disciples, and the disciples to those sitting
down; and likewise of the fish, as much as they wanted. So when they were filled, He said
to His disciples, "Gather up the fragments that remain, so that nothing is lost." Therefore
they gathered them up, and filled twelve baskets with the fragments of the five barley loaves
which were left over by those who had eaten. Then those men, when they had seen the sign
that Jesus did, said, "This is truly the Prophet who is to come into the world."*

John 6:10–14

Have you ever invited people to a dinner party, and when the doorbell rings,
you open the door and there stand many unexpected guests? Suddenly you're
keenly aware that the meal you have prepared is *not enough* to satiate the crowd
standing before you. Often we say to God, "Can't you see what's happening? Don't you know that I can't get through this situation?" as if He doesn't
already know or have power over our circumstances. We expect God to heed
our limited understanding when we say it's *not enough* to solve anything. In
our hands, bread and fish are not sufficient to feed five thousand, but there
is enough for twelve baskets full of leftovers in Jesus's hands. If we always go
with our plan, we may stifle the blessings in our lives. True disciples stick out
the rough times because they realize they have more than enough in Jesus
Christ. Repeating to ourselves that something is not enough only trains us to
deny the power of God. How can we expect God to step in and change our
lives when we continuously try to tell Him how to change it? God will bless
you when you trust Him with the results of your circumstances, regardless of
the present turmoil.

Father,

Whenever we are anxious about what is to come or what we need, remind us that You are our provider. You make ways to be who we are daily; some things we receive but never say thank-you for. Thank You, Lord. Thank You for the ways You help us even when we don't perceive it.

Amen.

DAY THIRTY-FOUR:

Breaking Free

So he went out and followed him, and did not know that what was done by the angel was real, but thought he was seeing a vision. When they were past the first and the second guard posts, they came to the iron gate that leads to the city, which opened to them of its own accord; and they went out and went down one street, and immediately the angel departed from him. And when Peter had come to himself, he said, "Now I know for certain that the Lord has sent His angel, and has delivered me from the hand of Herod and from all the expectation of the Jewish people."

Acts 12:9–11

There are times when our problems seem too much to handle. Disappointment sweeps in as the bills keep coming, our self-expectations are unmet, and time keeps ticking. What do we do when we feel shackled to our past, troubled by our present, and uncertain of our future? At times such as these, we need to surrender in prayer and trust to the knowledge and power of God. We must recognize that our human limitations are not the Lord's: in Him all things are possible. Peter himself didn't understand the process of *breaking free* until it was done. God broke him out of prison by sending an angel to guide him through. Once he was safely beyond the gates, he immediately acknowledged the miracle the Lord had done for him. When we think it is impossible to solve our problems, God can make a way out of no way. Our God is on our side, and we are no longer trapped in our past nor accountable to a future that isn't what He writes for us. This is your season to wake up and walk out the door opened for you.

Father,
We often feel that we are on the brink of a breakthrough. The things that had us bound in fear no longer matter, and we wish to rise to the occasion You called us to. If God be for us, who can be against us (Romans 8:31b)? Help us to remember this all the days of our lives as we leave behind what should have, could have, and would have destroyed us. Your love for us is all that matters ahead.

Amen.

DAY THIRTY-FIVE:

Walk Accordingly

If then you were raised with Christ, seek those things which are above, where Christ is, sitting at the right hand of God. Set your mind on things above, not on things on the earth. For you died, and your life is hidden with Christ in God. When Christ who is our life appears, then you also will appear with Him in glory. Therefore put to death your members which are on the earth: fornication, uncleanness, passion, evil desire, and covetousness, which is idolatry.

Colossians 3:1–5

When we choose to follow Jesus, He will come and abide in us, changing our past and molding us into what we should be. This can only be done by faith. However, faith is something that you absolutely cannot fake. No matter what darts, waves, flames, or taunts come your way, faith will keep your feet moving through obstacles. Believing in the name of Jesus is not some journey you take on for fun. It's a transformative journey to leave all the pain of your past, the crutches of your present, and the potholes of your future at the altar for Jesus to take care of. The glory of Jesus gets deep down into your spirit, changes your soul, renews your mind, and ultimately transforms your daily walk. When you let yourself rely on him, no one and nothing can stop you. Not even yourself. In our scripture today, we realize an essential truth: "For you died, and your life is hidden with Christ in God" (verse 3). When Jesus changes our lives, we will *walk according* to our faith; we will let our old selves pass away and get ready for the new experience. God is knocking at the door of your heart, prepared to change you if you let Him.

God,
You commanded the wind and the sea as quickly as You control our life circumstances. When You call us out of our old life, we beseech You to grow our trust in You so that we never waiver. Even if our emotions, common sense, or doubt try to throw us off course, let us continue our journey. Let Your word to us be enough for us to move through anything within our path.

Amen.

PART SIX:

Winning with Jesus

These things I have spoken to you, that in Me you may have peace.
In the world you will have tribulation; but be of good cheer,
I have overcome the world.

John 16:33

DAY THIRTY-SIX:

Blessed to Be with Jesus

Now it happened as they went that He entered a certain village; and a certain woman named Martha welcomed Him into her house. And she had a sister called Mary, who also sat at Jesus' feet and heard His word. But Martha was distracted with much serving, and she approached Him and said, "Lord, do You not care that my sister has left me to serve alone? Therefore tell her to help me." And Jesus answered and said to her, "Martha, Martha, you are worried and troubled about many things. But one thing is needed, and Mary has chosen that good part, which will not be taken away from her."

Luke 10:38–42

Got the napkins? Check. Is food ready? Check. Is the house clean? Double-check. Did you remember where to seat the guests? Absolutely. When we throw a party, we tend to go through all of the lists. Nothing feels worse than looking bad in front of a house full of people. What if they notice the floor-boards?! How on earth will we serve dinner on time?! As we shuffle around, making sure everything is perfect in our lives, we often forget the point of living. Worse yet, our quality time with Jesus falls through the cracks as we appease others. In the eyes of many, Martha wouldn't be wrong for asking Jesus to chastise Mary for not helping. However, in the kingdom of God, our priorities must be different. We must place God above everything and everyone else. If the King of Kings, the ruler of the universe, is sitting at your table, it doesn't matter what the placemats look like: spending time with Him should be your priority. As Christians, we've been invited to commune with God every day... and when we accept the invitation, we will find that we're *blessed to be with Jesus!*

God,
We tend to get busy in our day-to-day lives. Please help us to remain in Your presence. Our relationship with You supersedes our own need to feel validated at work. Keep us in Your company, and teach us to be still. Remind us what is important daily.

Amen.

DAY THIRTY-SEVEN:

Do the Right Thing

*Nebuchadnezzar spoke, saying to them, "Is it true, Shadrach, Meshach, and Abed-Nego,
that you do not serve my gods or worship the gold image which I have set up? Now if
you are ready at the time you hear the sound of the horn, flute, harp, lyre, and psaltery,
in symphony with all kinds of music, and you fall down and worship the image which I
have made, good! But if you do not worship, you shall be cast immediately into the midst
of a burning fiery furnace. And who is the god who will deliver you from my hands?"
Shadrach, Meshach, and Abed-Nego answered and said to the king, "O Nebuchadnezzar,
we have no need to answer you in this matter. If that is the case, our God whom we serve
is able to deliver us from the burning fiery furnace, and He will deliver us from your hand,
O king. But if not, let it be known to you, O king, that we do not serve your gods, nor will
we worship the gold image which you have set up."*

Daniel 3:14–18

As we discover our position and identity in Christ, we realize that who we
are is contrary to the world we live in. The world tells us to race to achieve
a perfect vision of ourselves, erected in the middle of the town square. The
house, the car, the bank account, the credibility, all to have everyone bow
and take notice. "Look how great they are—they've achieved so much," is
something we earnestly wish to hear. Then when we look at what we have
done for God and our fellow man, we come up empty. The truth is, integrity
is a much-needed character trait as we humbly follow Christ in this life. God
empowers us to be game-changers, standing up for what is right, not for our
gain, but Christ alone. Shadrach, Meshack, and Abed-Nego succeeded by
serving God with all they had. Giving in to Nebuchadnezzar would have
meant turning away from a lifetime relationship with God, to save their lives.
We should never be comfortable with pushing God aside. It won't be easy, and
the worldly fire you must endure will be hot, but remember God is right there
beside you when you *do the right thing*!

Lord,

We gratefully acknowledge Your presence at every turn in our lives. Let us walk in step with You daily to let others know who we serve. Challenge us to grow with Your Holy Spirit leading the way. No matter what the consequences are, let us see what real winning is about.

Amen.

DAY THIRTY-EIGHT:

No Shame

Then David returned to bless his household. And Michal the daughter of Saul came out to meet David, and said, "How glorious was the king of Israel today, uncovering himself today in the eyes of the maids of his servants, as one of the base fellows shamelessly uncovers himself!" So David said to Michal, " It was before the LORD, who chose me instead of your father and all his house, to appoint me ruler over the people of the LORD, over Israel. Therefore I will play music before the LORD. And I will be even more undignified than this, and will be humble in my own sight. But as for the maidservants of whom you have spoken, by them I will be held in honor." Therefore Michal the daughter of Saul had no children to the day of her death.

2 Samuel 6:20–23

Imagine walking down the street with your spouse and them refusing to hold your hand. They walk farther ahead, leaving you trailing behind while they pretend not to know you. A curtain of shame sweeps their face because they don't wish to seem to be in love with you. After returning home, they tell you, "I love you more than anything." The same thing happens when a person refuses to acknowledge God after a blessing. Singing gospel songs at the top of your lungs at church when you need His help, yet no one in public can tell you are Christian. For some, Christianity is acceptable, so long as it doesn't make others uncomfortable. Loving Jesus is excellent, so long as it fits your plan. In today's scripture, we realize that as publicly as God loves us, loving Him out loud is, at its simplest, just reciprocity. How often has God blessed your life? Have you praised Him enough? Remembering that Jesus saved us on the cross should encourage you to worship Him with *no shame*.

Lord,
Encourage us to be unashamed in our love for You. No matter how high You take us or who is watching, let us at a moment's notice humble ourselves to love and adore You. Give us the strength to praise when we don't feel like it and the audacity to dance when we do.

Amen.

DAY THIRTY-NINE:

Praise in Advance

"Then I said to you, 'Do not be terrified, or afraid of them. The LORD your God, who goes before you, He will fight for you, according to all He did for you in Egypt before your eyes, and in the wilderness where you saw how the LORD your God carried you, as a man carries his son, in all the way that you went until you came to this place.' Yet, for all that, you did not believe the LORD your God, who went in the way before you to search out a place for you to pitch your tents, to show you the way you should go, in the fire by night and in the cloud by day.

"And the LORD heard the sound of your words, and was angry, and took an oath, saying, 'Surely not one of these men of this evil generation shall see that good land of which I swore to give to your fathers, except Caleb the son of Jephunneh; he shall see it, and to him and his children I am giving the land on which he walked, because he wholly followed the LORD.'"

Deuteronomy 1:29–36

On the precipice of change, two conflicting ideas occur. The first thought is that whatever awaits on the other side has the raw potential to destroy everything you have come to know. The second thought is a smaller, yet stiller, resolve that God never changes no matter what happens on the other side. As believers in Jesus, we must remind ourselves of the goodness of the Lord. When we recall the victories that God has given us, we are free to rely on our faith to take us to the other side. We don't have to know all of the details; we are assured that the God that brought us here is still for us. We don't have time to pay attention to the potential of disappointment while we press toward our blessings. Instead of using your time to fret over something God said you would overcome, praise, and thank Him for the victory. It is better to celebrate what God has promised than to lament what you think won't happen. Don't limit God by your unbelief; raise your expectations, *praise Him in advance*, and watch Him deliver results.

Lord,

You have the ultimate perspective on all of our circumstances. As we choose to walk with You on this journey, inspire us to see our lives in victory. Help us to ignore the negativity we hear and embrace the destiny You set out for us.

Amen.

DAY FORTY:

Believe It

Now Thomas, called the Twin, one of the twelve, was not with them when Jesus came. The other disciples therefore said to him, "We have seen the Lord." So he said to them, "Unless I see in His hands the print of the nails, and put my finger into the print of the nails, and put my hand into His side, I will not believe." And after eight days His disciples were again inside, and Thomas with them. Jesus came, the doors being shut, and stood in the midst, and said, "Peace to you!" Then He said to Thomas, "Reach your finger here, and look at My hands; and reach your hand here, and put it into My side. Do not be unbelieving, but believing." And Thomas answered and said to Him, "My Lord and my God!" Jesus said to him, "Thomas, because you have seen Me, you have believed. Blessed are those who have not seen and yet have believed.""

John 20:24–29

Everyone can appreciate a great story. The thrill, adventure, danger, and victories told in bold words and eloquent speech intrigues us, but there is nothing quite like living one yourself. A million stories cannot add up to the one you live daily. No action could match reaching out to touch the print of nails for yourself. Thomas is as questioning as any of us would be at the thought of a dead man walking. He knew of the death of Christ— but to see Him get back up? Unbelievable. When you get on your knees to pray, do you expect an answer? When you look over your life, do you see the marks where Christ has touched it? After witnessing a miracle, there is nothing left to do but be grateful. When blessings, mercy, or grace is given to you, live it. Enjoy it. Appreciate it. You have a rare front-row seat to the majesty of God. You know by your own life's story that Jesus walks with you. Thomas was blessed to see Jesus after the cross. In our lives, we are even more blessed to receive Him in our hearts… without that moment. We've never seen Jesus's face personally, but the signature on our life is all His. Praise God for the ability to *believe it!*

Jesus,

You know how difficult it is to dare to believe in this world. Teach us, Lord, how steadfast You are. Declare Your promises over our lives. Give us the strength to own up to our doubts and then be honest in overcoming them. Instill in us an unwavering faith and a will to believe that lasts a lifetime.

Amen.

What would
you Dare
to Believe?

Daring Believer
Self-Check

I Believe God for:

_____

_____

_____

_____

_____

_____

_____

_____

_____

_____

_____

_____

_____

_____

_____

_____

_____

_____

_____

_____

_____

_____

_____

What Has God Called Me To Do?

_____

_____

_____

_____

_____

_____

_____

_____

_____

_____

_____

_____

_____

_____

_____

_____

_____

_____

_____

_____

_____

_____

_____

_____

_____

_____

How can I better serve God's plan?

_____

_____

_____

_____

_____

_____

_____

_____

_____

_____

_____

_____

_____

_____

_____

_____

_____

_____

_____

_____

_____

_____

_____

_____

How have I changed in this journey with Christ?

_____

_____

_____

_____

_____

_____

_____

_____

_____

_____

_____

_____

_____

_____

_____

_____

_____

_____

_____

_____

_____

_____

_____

_____

_____

_____

What battles have I overcome with Jesus?

_____

_____

_____

_____

_____

_____

_____

_____

_____

_____

_____

_____

_____

_____

_____

_____

_____

_____

_____

_____

_____

_____

_____

What will I choose to do in Good and Bad times?

_____

_____

_____

_____

_____

_____

_____

_____

_____

_____

_____

_____

_____

_____

_____

_____

_____

_____

_____

_____

_____

_____

Daring Believer Notes

I Dare To: _____

_____

_____

_____

_____

_____

_____

_____

_____

_____

_____

_____

_____

_____

_____

_____

_____

_____

_____

_____

_____

_____

_____

_____

_____

_____

_____

_____

_____

_____

_____

_____

_____

_____

_____

_____

ACKNOWLEDGMENTS

I owe this book and any other success in life to my Lord and Savior, Jesus Christ. I know that may sound cliché, but in all reality, God gave me enough strength to believe in this devotional. As a youth, I would scribble in endless notebooks and dream of a day I would share a story worth telling. I could never have dreamed that God would inspire me to work on *Daring Believer*. I thank God for ushering in great mentors and family members along the way who encouraged me to pursue this wholeheartedly. He continually placed me in the right rooms to learn from the best and be daring about what I believed. When I volunteered to work for the church and online ministries, I desired to share what I learned throughout the years. I thank my husband, Gregory Hacker, for being on my cheer team. Whether it was late nights thinking about topics or mornings reading the Bible, he made it a priority to encourage me. My mother, who is not only a spectacular deacon but an excellent reader, gave me her vote of confidence during the editing phase. She is an integral inspiration for my faith walk, and I aspire to make Mama Bear proud. My sister Sharika always believed I would write books, even before I could see that talent within myself. Her prodding when I was younger, and even now, gives me the continual motivation to put pen to paper. My father has given me solid advice before every significant moment in my life. Before writing this devotional, he told me, "Never leave anything on the table. Do what you set out to do, and you will never have regrets." I wrote this devotional intending to put everything I had out there for Jesus. I never wanted to leave anything unsaid, and for those wise words, I am grateful. I am thankful for every triumph, defeat, twist, and turn on my journey with God. If I could go through my life all over again, I would, just to know Him. Everything from the people, places, and things in my life, He fashioned together for my good. So, if I did not mention your name, just know I am grateful for you as well.

ABOUT THE AUTHOR

Tameka M. Hacker was born in Honolulu, Hawaii, raised in northern Virginia, and forged in the church. As a deacon's child, ministry volunteer, and choir singer, she is no stranger to church life. As a woman of God, Tameka is fire-tested and battle-proven through the trenches of life. Having experienced everything from martial arts championships to multicultural galas, she uses her triumphs and her disappointments to relate on a whole new level. She has a Master's of Science in Strategic Public Relations and has traveled the world with her husband, Gregory. Having a story worth telling, this author devotes her life to encouraging others to see themselves the way God does.